Be Water Wise

Contents

written by John Lockyer

1

Water is part of our lives every day.
We drink it and cook with it. We use it to wash
our clothes, our dishes, and ourselves. We play
in it, swim in it, and use it to water our gardens.

2

We need water for many different things. Because it's so easy to use, sometimes we forget that it is precious. Where does our water come from?

There is a lot of water on our planet. Most of the Earth is covered by oceans. But water from the ocean is very salty, so it can't be used for drinking, washing, or watering plants.

We know that water falls to Earth as rain. Most of the water we use comes from under the ground. The rest of it comes from lakes, rivers, and streams. How does water get to our homes?

Dams are built across rivers to hold back
the water. Big drills are used to reach water
underground. Then it is pumped to the surface
and stored in huge reservoirs.

After the water is cleaned, it's pumped through big pipes to reach our homes. When we want to use water, all we have to do is turn on a tap. Why do we need to save water?

Every year the number of people living on Earth gets bigger. All of these people need water to live. In some countries where there is less rainfall, there isn't enough water to drink or grow food.

Most of the water that comes to our homes goes down the drain after we have used it. Water is precious, so we must all try to find ways to use water wisely.
How can we save water?

We must always turn the water off tightly because drips can waste a lot of water. It's better to keep a bottle of drinking water in the refrigerator than to run the water until it gets cold.

We shouldn't put any more water than we need in the sink when we wash dishes or clean vegetables. We should have a short shower instead of a bath.

There are good ways to save water outside your home.
The best way to water your garden is with a watering
can. If you use a hose, it is better to hold it in your
hand than to leave it running.

12

It is wise to use a bucket of water when you clean your bike or car. You can wash your pet without wasting water, too!

Use this quiz to check how water wise you are:
Does a bath or a shower use more water?
When you have a wash, should you keep the tap
running or turn it off?

How much water should we put in the kitchen sink?
What is the best way to save water when you want
to have a cold drink of water?

How can we stop wasting water outside our homes? Learn how to help save water. Be water wise!